P9-BZR-551

George Washington

by Erin Edison

Consulting Editor: Gail Saunders-Smith, PhD

Consultant:
Sheila Blackford
Librarian, Scripps Library
Managing Editor, *American President*
Miller Center, University of Virginia

CAPSTONE PRESS
a capstone imprint

Pebble Plus is published by Capstone Press,
1710 Roe Crest Drive, North Mankato, Minnesota 56003.
www.capstonepub.com

Library of Congress Cataloging-in-Publication Data
Edison, Erin.
  George Washington / by Erin Edison.
      p. cm.
  Includes bibliographical references and index.
  Summary: "Simple text and full-color photographs describe the life of George Washington"—Provided by publisher.
  ISBN 978-1-4296-8737-9 (library binding)
  ISBN 978-1-62065-319-7 (ebook PDF)
  1. Washington, George, 1732-1799—Juvenile literature. 2. Presidents—United States—Biography—Juvenile
literature. I. Title.
  E312.66.E33 2013
  973.4'1092—dc23
  [B]   2011049981

Editorial Credits
Erika L. Shores, editor; Sarah Bennett, designer; Wanda Winch, media researcher; Kathy McColley,
      production specialist

Photo Credits
Alamy: North Wind Picture Archives, 11, 15, 17, Pictorial Press Ltd., 5; Corbis: Bettmann, 7, Museum of the City
of New York, cover, PoodlesRock, 13; Dreamstime: Richie Lomba, 1, 21; Library of Congress: Prints and Photographs
Division, 9, 19

Note to Parents and Teachers

The Presidential Biographies series supports national history standards related to people and
culture. This book describes and illustrates the life of George Washington. The images support
early readers in understanding the text. The repetition of words and phrases helps early readers
learn new words. This book also introduces early readers to subject-specific vocabulary words,
which are defined in the Glossary section. Early readers may need assistance to read some
words and to use the Table of Contents, Glossary, Read More, Internet Sites, and Index sections
of the book.

Printed in the United States of America in North Mankato, Minnesota.
062013   007381R

Table of Contents

Early Life

George Washington was the first president of the United States.

He was born February 22, 1732.

He grew up on a Virginia farm.

George went to school for a short time, but he mostly studied at home.

born in Westmoreland County, Virginia

1732

4

painting of George's birthplace in Westmoreland County, Virginia

5

Young Adult

George began to work as

a surveyor when he was 16.

He measured land in Virginia.

George made some of the first

maps of Virginia. At age 20,

George joined the Virginia militia.

born in Westmoreland
County, Virginia

1732

1752

joins Virginia
militia

In 1759 George married
Martha Custis. She and
her two children came
to live with George.
They lived at his plantation
called Mount Vernon.

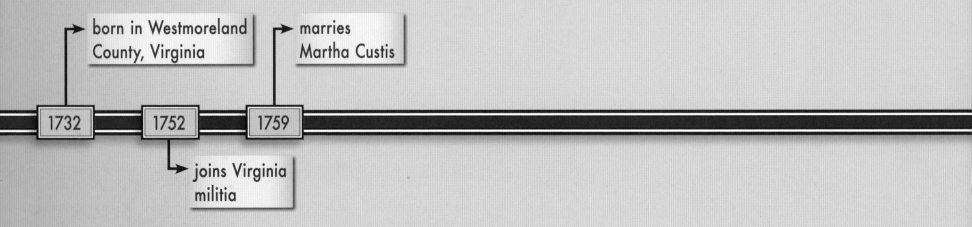

born in Westmoreland
County, Virginia

marries
Martha Custis

| 1732 | 1752 | 1759 |

joins Virginia
militia

9

The Revolutionary War

The Revolutionary War began
in 1775. George led the army
of American colonists.
They fought a long and hard war
against Great Britain.

born in Westmoreland
County, Virginia

marries
Martha Custis

| 1732 | 1752 | 1759 | 1775 |

joins Virginia
militia

Revolutionary War
begins

The colonists won the war in 1783. They formed a new country called the United States of America. George returned to Mount Vernon after the war.

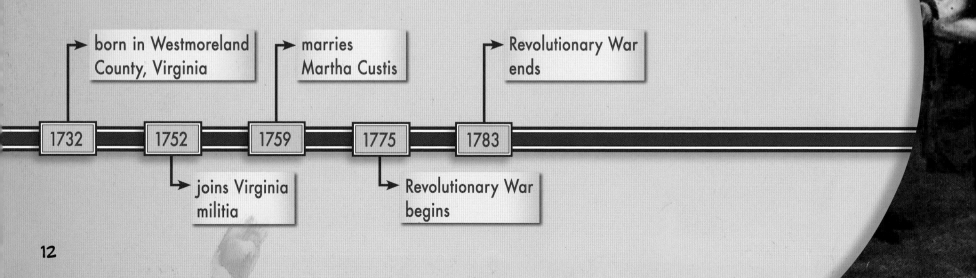

born in Westmoreland County, Virginia

marries Martha Custis

Revolutionary War ends

| 1732 | 1752 | 1759 | 1775 | 1783 |

joins Virginia militia

Revolutionary War begins

George Washington

In this painting, George watches as the British surrender at Yorktown.

President Washington

George became the first president
of the United States in 1789.
George helped plan the capital city,
Washington, D.C., which was
named for him.

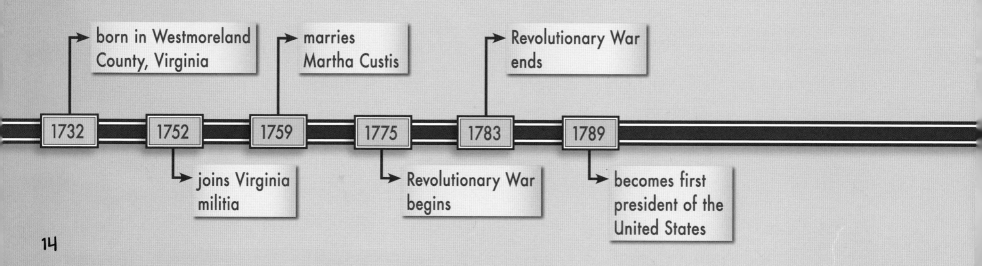

born in Westmoreland County, Virginia

marries Martha Custis

Revolutionary War ends

1732   1752   1759   1775   1783   1789

joins Virginia militia

Revolutionary War begins

becomes first president of the United States

As president, George worked on problems facing the new country. He signed treaties with American Indians and other countries. George set up many parts of the U.S. government. He helped make the court system.

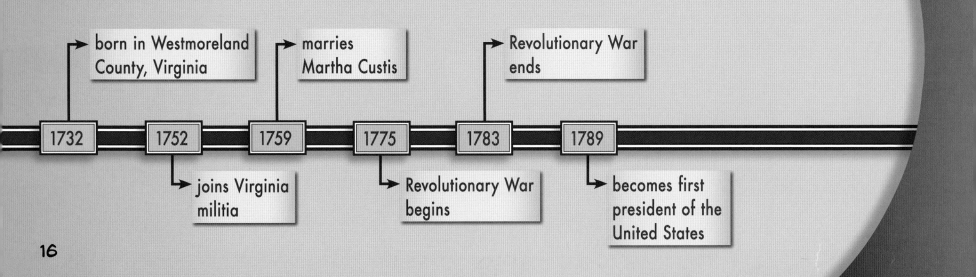

born in Westmoreland County, Virginia

marries Martha Custis

Revolutionary War ends

| 1732 | 1752 | 1759 | 1775 | 1783 | 1789 |

joins Virginia militia

Revolutionary War begins

becomes first president of the United States

George was president
for eight years. Many people
wanted him to serve longer,
but he said no.
He returned to his home
at Mount Vernon.

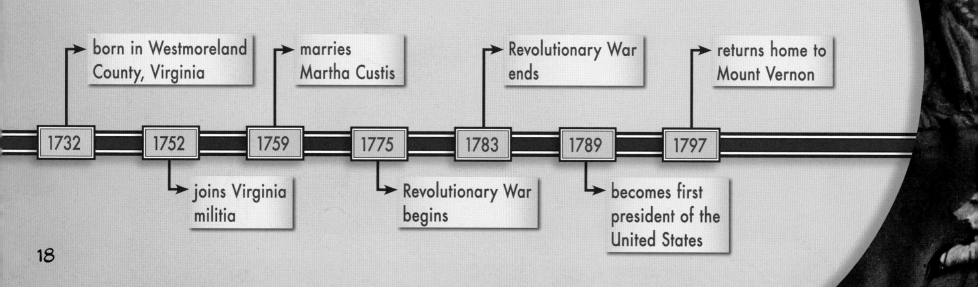

born in Westmoreland
County, Virginia

marries
Martha Custis

Revolutionary War
ends

returns home to
Mount Vernon

1732   1752   1759   1775   1783   1789   1797

joins Virginia
militia

Revolutionary War
begins

becomes first
president of the
United States

Remembering Washington

George died at Mount Vernon
on December 14, 1799.
George fought for and helped
shape the United States.
Americans remember him as
the "Father of His Country."

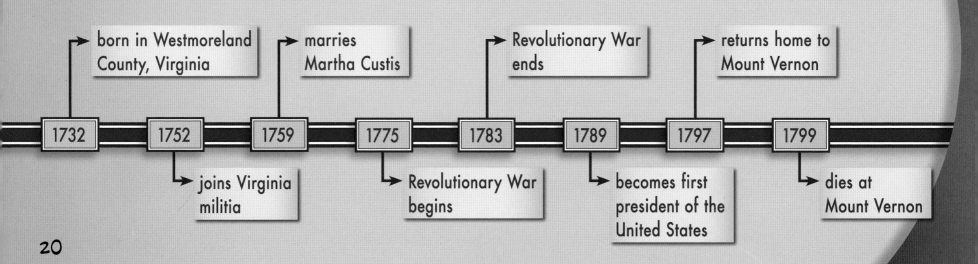

born in Westmoreland County, Virginia

marries Martha Custis

Revolutionary War ends

returns home to Mount Vernon

1732 1752 1759 1775 1783 1789 1797 1799

joins Virginia militia

Revolutionary War begins

becomes first president of the United States

dies at Mount Vernon

Glossary

capital—a city where a country's government is based

colonist—a person who lives in a colony; a colony is land ruled by another country

militia—a group of citizens who have been organized to fight as a group but who are not professional soldiers

plantation—a large farm where one main crop is grown

Revolutionary War—the war in which the 13 American colonies won their independence from Great Britain

surveyor—a person who measures land and makes maps

treaty—a written agreement between countries or groups of people

Read More

Allen, Kathy. *President George Washington.* Our American Story. Minneapolis: Picture Window Books, 2010.

Gosman, Gillian. *George Washington.* Life Stories. New York: PowerKids Press, 2011.

Lee, Sally. *Martha Washington.* First Ladies. Mankato, Minn.: Capstone Press, 2011.

Internet Sites

FactHound offers a safe, fun way to find Internet sites related to this book. All of the sites on FactHound have been researched by our staff.

Here's all you do:

Visit *www.facthound.com*

Type in this code: 9781429687379

Check out projects, games and lots more at
www.capstonekids.com

Index

Word Count: 253
Grade: 1
Early-Intervention Level: 23

24